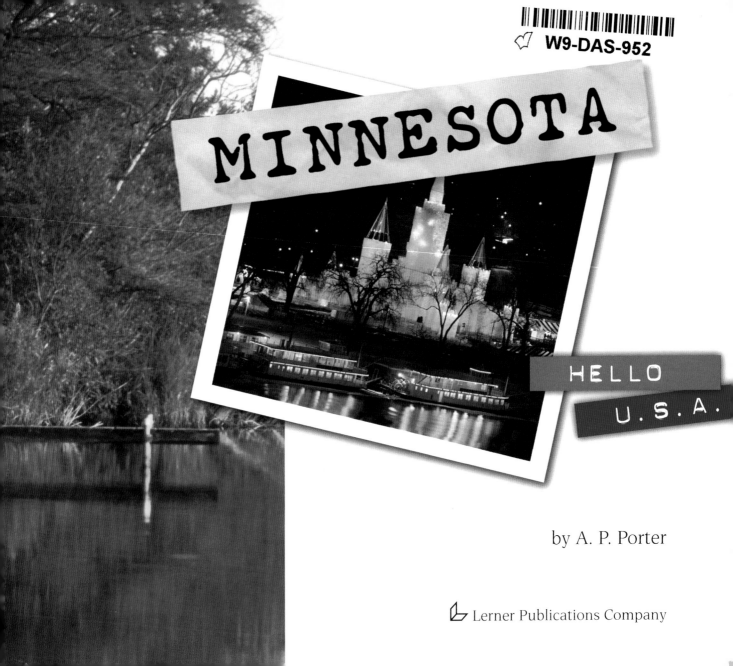

MINNESOTA

HELLO

U.S.A.

by A. P. Porter

Lerner Publications Company

You'll find this picture of agates at the beginning of each chapter. These stones are found in northern Minnesota. The red and orange bands on the stones come from the iron ore in the area's soil. Minnesota's state gemstone is the Lake Superior agate.

Cover (left): Cross-country skier near Grand Marais. Cover (right): Mall of America in Bloomington. Pages 2–3: Dock on lake near Park Rapids. Page 3: Ice Palace at the Saint Paul Winter Carnival.

Copyright © 2002 by Lerner Publications Company

This book is available in two editions:
Library binding by Lerner Publications Company, a division of Lerner Publishing Group
Soft cover by First Avenue Editions, an imprint of Lerner Publishing Group
241 First Avenue North
Minneapolis, MN 55401 U.S.A.

Website address: www.lernerbooks.com

LIBRARY OF CONGRESS CATALOGING-IN-PUBLICATION DATA

Porter, A. P.
    Minnesota / by A. P. Porter (Rev. and expanded 2nd ed.)
       p. cm. — (Hello U.S.A.)
    Includes index.
    Summary: Introduces the geography, history, industries, people, and other highlights of Minnesota
    ISBN 0-8225-4059-2 (lib. bdg.: alk. paper)
    ISBN 0-8225-4149-1 (pbk.: alk. paper)
     1. Minnesota—Juvenile literature. [1. Minnesota] I. Title. II. Series.
    F606.3.P67 2002
    977.6—dc21   2001002447

Manufactured in the United States of America
1 2 3 4 5 6 – JR – 07 06 05 04 03 02

CONTENTS

Minnesotans enjoy the state's many lakes during both summer and winter. Ice fishing is popular on Mille Lacs Lake in east central Minnesota.

THE LAND

10,000 Lakes and More

Minnesota, nicknamed the Star of the North, lies in the heart of North America. By land area, it is the second largest state in the Midwest. Minnesota is bordered on the east by Wisconsin and on the west by North and South Dakota. Canada is to Minnesota's north, and Iowa is to its south. The waters of Lake Superior, one of the five **Great Lakes,** lap against Minnesota's northeastern boundary.

Glaciers covered much of Minnesota about 10,000 years ago, during the last **ice age.** By the time these slowly moving masses of ice and packed snow had melted, they had flattened much of Minnesota's land.

Blazing star is a wildflower found in Minnesota and its midwestern neighbors.

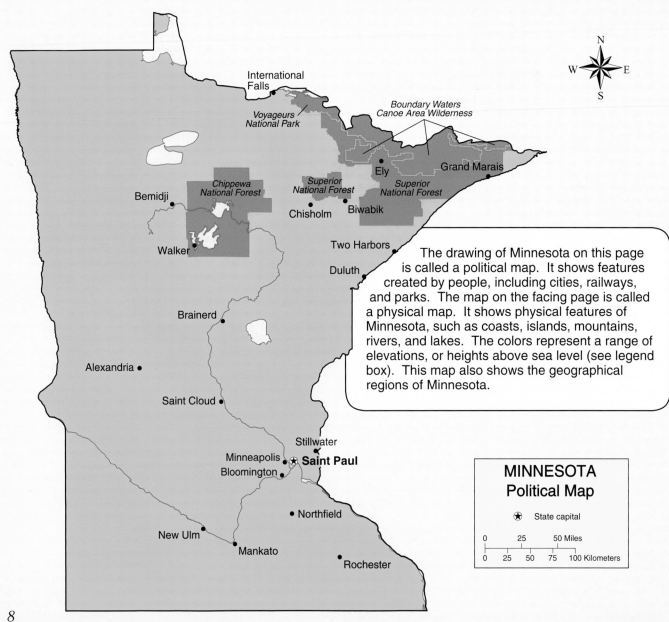

International
Falls

*Voyageurs
National Park*

*Boundary Waters
Canoe Area Wilderness*

Ely

Grand Marais

Bemidji

*Chippewa
National Forest*

*Superior
National Forest*

*Superior
National Forest*

Chisholm

Biwabik

Walker

Two Harbors

Duluth

The drawing of Minnesota on this page is called a political map. It shows features created by people, including cities, railways, and parks. The map on the facing page is called a physical map. It shows physical features of Minnesota, such as coasts, islands, mountains, rivers, and lakes. The colors represent a range of elevations, or heights above sea level (see legend box). This map also shows the geographical regions of Minnesota.

Brainerd

Alexandria

Saint Cloud

Stillwater

Minneapolis ⭐ **Saint Paul**

Bloomington

Northfield

New Ulm

Mankato

Rochester

MINNESOTA
Political Map

⭐ State capital

0		25		50 Miles
0	25	50	75	100 Kilometers

N
W E
S

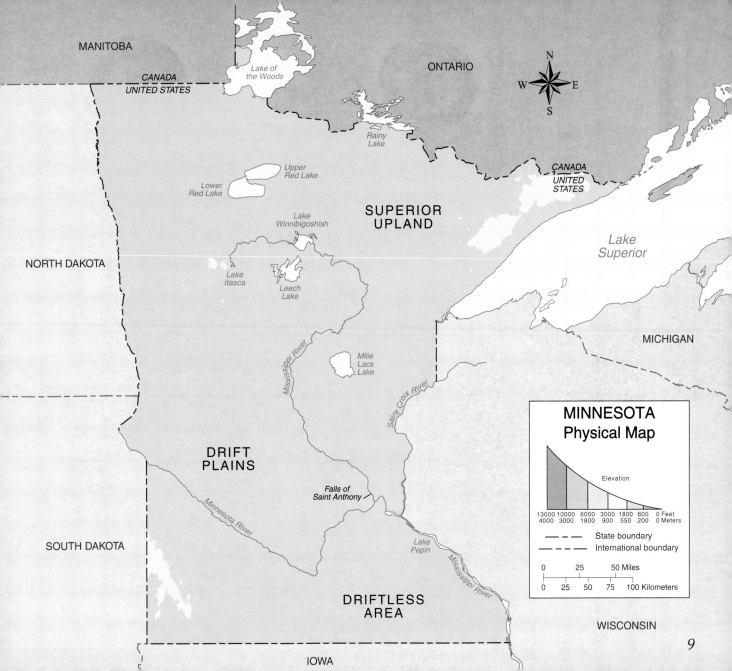

MANITOBA

Lake of the Woods

CANADA
UNITED STATES

ONTARIO

N
W E
S

Rainy Lake

CANADA
UNITED STATES

Upper Red Lake

Lower Red Lake

SUPERIOR UPLAND

NORTH DAKOTA

Lake Winnibigoshish

Lake Superior

Lake Itasca

Leech Lake

Mille Lacs Lake

MICHIGAN

Mississippi River

Saint Croix River

DRIFT PLAINS

Minnesota River

Falls of Saint Anthony

SOUTH DAKOTA

Lake Pepin

Mississippi River

DRIFTLESS AREA

WISCONSIN

IOWA

MINNESOTA
Physical Map

Elevation

13000 10000 6000 3000 1800 600 0 Feet
4000 3000 1800 900 550 200 0 Meters

State boundary
International boundary

0   25   50 Miles
0   25   50   75   100 Kilometers

9

The glaciers left Minnesota with three geographic regions. They are the Superior Upland, the Drift Plains, and the Driftless Area.

The Superior Upland covers much of the northern half of Minnesota. The region is rugged and dotted with boulders. As the glaciers scraped across Minnesota, they gouged holes that later filled with water. In the northeastern corner of the state, these glacial lakes are called the Boundary Waters because they form the boundary between Minnesota and Canada.

By area Lake Superior is the largest body of fresh water in the world. In Minnesota it meets the eastern edge of the Superior Upland.

The Drift Plains, which lie south and west of the Superior Upland, cover almost half of Minnesota. Glaciers ground down the land in this region and left **drift,** or rich topsoil, as they melted.

The Driftless Area is in the southeastern corner of Minnesota. The region is driftless because glaciers never reached the area to flatten it and deposit drift. Instead, steep **bluffs** overlook deep river valleys.

Towering bluffs line rivers in southeastern Minnesota.

Glaciers formed thousands of lakes within Minnesota. In fact, another state nickname is the Land of 10,000 Lakes. Minnesota actually has about 15,000 lakes. The largest of these are Upper and Lower Red Lake, Lake Winnibigoshish, Leech Lake, and Mille Lacs Lake.

Many Minnesotans spend their free time at the state's lakes.

The Mississippi River, the longest river in the United States, begins at Lake Itasca in northern

Young Minnesotans enjoy playing in the snow during winter.

Minnesota. Most of the state's major rivers—including the Minnesota and the Saint Croix—flow into the mighty Mississippi.

Minnesota is famous for its cold winters, but the state has four seasons and a wide range of temperatures. In July, average temperatures are 68° F in the north and 74° F in the south. In January, average temperatures are 2° F in the north and 15° F in the south.

Snowstorms and bone-chilling winds are common throughout the state during the winter. An average of 70 inches of snow falls in northeastern Minnesota every year. Eastern Minnesota receives the most rain and snow in the state. The climate gets drier toward the west.

Northern Minnesota's climate is ideal for pine and birch trees *(left)*. Minnesotans and visitors explore Minnesota's woods during the fall to see the colorful leaves *(below)*.

More than one-third of Minnesota is forested, mostly in the north. Pine, spruce, balsam, fir, aspen, and white birch trees grow there. In the pine forests, honeysuckle, wintergreen, trailing arbutus, and blueberries thrive in sunny spots. Maple, black walnut, oak, and other hardwood trees fill woodlands in the south.

Much of Minnesota was once covered with prairie. These vast grasslands had grass so tall that early explorers had to stand on the backs of their horses to see over it. Most of the prairie has been plowed to raise wheat, corn, and other crops, but prairie wildflowers such as blazing stars and asters still flourish.

Unlike many other states, Minnesota is home to several kinds of large wild animals. Most of Minnesota's wildlife lives in the northern part of the state, where people are much more scarce. Moose and black bears, along with otters, snapping turtles, bald eagles, and even timber wolves, live in the swamps and woods of the north.

Timber wolves roam parts of northern Minnesota.

Great blue heron

Mink, white-tailed deer, and beavers live throughout Minnesota. Red foxes and raccoons can sometimes be found even in the state's large cities.

Minnesota's thousands of lakes are havens for ducks and geese. Mallard ducks flock to Minnesota's **wetlands.** Anglers cast their hooks for bass, walleye, northern pike, trout, catfish, and muskellunge.

A Rich Heritage

he first people to come to the region that later became Minnesota probably arrived about 10,000 years ago. They were big-game hunters from northeastern Asia who tracked their food supply—giant bison and mammoths—across a land bridge that once connected Asia and North America. A few spear points chipped from rock are almost all that remain of these ancient people.

When the big-game hunters came, the climate was getting warmer and the glaciers were melting. As the temperature became more bearable, the lives of these early North Americans became easier. The descendants of the first people, called Native Americans or Indians, began picking fruit and nuts and hunting squirrels, rabbits, and other small animals.

Wild berries and nuts were important foods for early Native Americans in Minnesota.

Long ago, Native Americans who lived near the swamps and lakes of northern and central Minnesota harvested wild rice from shallow waters. Some Native Americans still practice this tradition.

About 500 years ago, an Indian people called the Dakota, which means "friend," were the only people living where the prairies of the Drift Plains meet the forests of the Superior Upland. In the summer, the Dakota lived in houses made of bark and wooden poles. They hunted elk, deer, and buffalo, drying part of the meat supply for winter. Then they lived in tepees made of hides.

When Native Americans hunted in the winter, they wore snowshoes. This way, they could move quickly over deep snow.

In the 1650s, French explorers Pierre Esprit Radisson and Médard Chouart des Groseilliers traveled to the northwestern shore of Lake Superior. They were probably the first white people in the region.

In 1680 Louis Hennepin, a **missionary** from Belgium, visited the site that later became the city of Minneapolis. Hennepin was the first European known to have reached this area. More explorers and traders followed. Some were looking for a water route to the Pacific Ocean. Most came to make money.

The Indians traded furs to the French for items such as cloth, needles, thread, guns, and iron kettles. The French sold the furs at a great profit in Europe and Asia, where fur hats were popular.

While Louis Hennepin was exploring the area that later became Minnesota, he was captured by Indians. The Indians led their captive past a waterfall on the Mississippi River. Hennepin named it the Falls of Saint Anthony.

The lakes and rivers of northern Minnesota served as highways for fur traders. When the traders arrived at land, they carried their canoes and supplies to the next body of water.

In the late 1600s, Native Americans called the Ojibway were moving into the northern and eastern lands of the Dakota people. The Ojibway were being pushed westward by the Iroquois Indians, who had been pushed westward by European settlers from North America's eastern coast.

French fur traders became rich from selling the thick pelts of otters and other animals *(above)*. At trading posts, fur traders exchanged their furs for food, money, or other supplies *(opposite page)*.

The Dakota agreed to let the Ojibway stay and hunt. In return, the Dakota wanted the Ojibway to let French traders from the Great Lakes pass through Ojibway country to trade with the Dakota. The Ojibway agreed.

The pelts of otters, muskrat, and especially beavers were the furs most valued by the French. These animals grew their thickest fur in the cold north, where the Ojibway had settled. The Dakota (called Sioux by the French) wanted to live again where they could trap the best furs for trade.

The Ojibway and Dakota started fighting each other in 1736. Gradually, the Ojibway pushed the Dakota to the south and west. By 1800 the Ojibway controlled all of what later became northern Minnesota. The Dakota still held the south, though, and the place they called *Mdo-te*, later "Mendota," became a trading center for furs and other goods.

In 1803 France sold a huge area of land in central North America to the United States. This deal, called the Louisiana Purchase, included most of Minnesota. The Louisiana Purchase doubled the size of the United States. But the Indians living in the area knew nothing of this and believed that they were free to live and hunt there.

In 1805 explorer and U.S. Army officer Zebulon Pike was sent to Mendota, at the junction of the Mississippi and Minnesota Rivers. Representing the U.S. government, Pike traded with the Dakota for land on which to build a fort. Fort Snelling, built there in 1820, was the first government outpost in the region.

Soldiers stationed at Fort Snelling built a sawmill upstream at the Falls of Saint Anthony. The soldiers cut down trees, using them as firewood and as lumber for fences and buildings. The army planted wheat and built a mill to grind the grain into flour.

By the time the fort was completed in 1824, buffalo and

Many of Minnesota's early buildings were built with lumber cut from the state's large forests.

Minnesota's first hospital and first school were located at Fort Snelling.

other animals the Indians hunted had become scarce in the area. With their source of food gone, the Dakota and the Ojibway sold their lands east of the Mississippi River to the U.S. government in 1837. Americans and Europeans began to settle on the former Indian lands. They founded the towns of Stillwater, Saint Anthony (which later became Minneapolis), and Saint Paul.

Lumber companies came to the Saint Croix River valley, where trees were abundant. Saint Paul, on the Mississippi River, became a major fur market.

Trappers brought furs to Saint Paul from all over the region. Some pelts arrived from the north in carts pulled by oxen or ponies. The clumsy carts took up to two months to get to Saint Paul. Steam-powered paddle wheelers carried pelts and lumber from Saint Paul and brought back paper, cloth, furniture, live-stock, and food—supplies needed by the settlers.

By the mid-1800s, Saint Paul was a busy port. In 1849 the city became the capital of the Minnesota Territory.

In 1851 Dakota leaders signed **treaties** selling most of southern Minnesota to the United States. Unable to read and write English, Indian leaders also signed away some of the money they should

have received under the treaty of 1837. The Ojibway signed over almost all of the northern half of Minnesota in the treaties of 1854 and 1855.

About 8,000 Dakota moved to a narrow strip of land along the Minnesota River. Most of the Ojibway agreed to live on small **reservations,** areas of land set aside for them, in northern Minnesota.

Immigrants from Germany, Ireland, Sweden, and Norway swarmed into the Minnesota Territory. Settlers soon vastly outnumbered the fewer than 20,000 Native Americans left in the area. In 1855 Minnesota had 40,000 white people. By 1857 there were 150,000. And by 1858 Minnesota had enough people to become the 32nd state in the Union.

In 1851 Dakota leaders and U.S. government officials met to sign treaties. The Indians received only a few cents for each acre of land they sold to the government.

U.S.-Dakota Conflict of 1862

During the summer of 1862, the Dakota Indians were living on a narrow strip of land along the Minnesota River. Wildlife was scarce. Last year's crop had been ruined by cutworms, this year's crop was not ready, and the traders would not give the Indians food and goods. The government was late with their annual payment for the land they had bought from the Dakota. Without that money, the Indians could not buy food. It seemed as though the Dakota had sold their homeland for nothing.

The Dakota were starving to death. Settlers who lived nearby refused to give them food. The whites assumed that the Indians would be taken care of by the government or else thought that it was their own fault if they were suffering. Some Indians, hoping to take back their land, persuaded a Dakota chief named Little Crow (pictured) to lead them in a war against the white settlers.

Little Crow expected the Dakota to lose the war, and in only a few weeks they did. Nearly 600 people, counting white settlers, soldiers, and Indians, were killed in the fighting. Thirty-eight Dakota who were charged with murder were hanged in Mankato after the war. Hundreds more Dakota were sent to prison or were forced to leave their homes in Minnesota and resettle on barren land in South Dakota. Little Crow fled Minnesota during the war but was killed when he returned in 1863.

More than 100 years later, the state of Minnesota and the Dakota people declared 1987 the Year of Reconciliation. The state recognized that both the settlers and the Dakota had true complaints in the conflict. At a ceremony in Mankato honoring the 38 American Indians who were hanged, eagles—meant to stand for spirits—were seen flying overhead.

For years, Northern and Southern states in the Union had been disagreeing over many issues, including whether Southerners should own slaves. To make sure slavery would still be legal, the Southern states decided to leave the Union. In 1861 they formed their own country, called the Confederate States of America. When Confederate troops attacked a Union fort, the Civil War began. Minnesota was the first state to offer troops to the Union.

After the Civil War, some former slaves left the South for states that had supported the Union. Some of them joined the U.S. Army. These soldiers were stationed at Fort Snelling.

The Civil War ended with a Union victory in 1865. Minnesota turned to building railroads and flour mills. Trains hauled Minnesota's flour, lumber, and farm goods to the East Coast. Minnesota got one of its nicknames, the Gopher State, from a newspaper cartoon that pictured gophers pulling a train across gopher-filled prairies.

In the 1860s, the U.S. government passed the Homestead Act. This law promised free land in Minnesota and other western territories to almost anyone willing to farm it. Minnesotans advertised abroad for people to make Minnesota their home. Norwegians, Swedes, Germans, and Finns came to plow up the land that had once belonged to the Dakota people.

3000 LABORERS
WANTED

On the LAKE SUPERIOR AND MISSISSIPPI RAILROAD from Duluth at the Western Extremity of Lake Superior, to ST PAUL

Constant Employment will be given. Wages range from $2.00 to $4.00 per Day.

MECHANICS
Are Needed at Duluth!

Wages to Masons and Plasterers, $4.00 per day; Carpenters, $3.00 per day.

10,000 EMIGRANTS

WANTED TO SETTLE ON THE LANDS OF THE COMPANY, NOW OFFERED ON LIBERAL CREDITS AND AT LOW PRICES.

Large bodies of Government Lands, subject to *Homestead* Settlement, or open to *Pre-Emption.* These Lands offer Facilities to Settlers not surpassed, if equalled by any lands in the West. They lie *right along the line* of the Railroad connecting Lake Superior with the Mississippi River, one of the most important Roads in the West. Forty miles of the Road are now in running order, and the whole Road (150 miles) will be completed by June, 1870. WHITE and YELLOW PINE, and VALUABLE HARDWOOD, convenient to Market, abound.

The SOIL is admirably adapted to the raising of WINTER WHEAT and TAME GRASSES. *Stock have Good Pasture until the Depth of Winter.*

The waters of Lake Superior, in connection with the Timber, make this much the warmest part of Minnesota. The navigation season at Duluth is several weeks longer than on the Mississippi. The LUMBER interest will furnish abundant and profitable *WINTER WORK.*

FREE TRANSPORTATION over the completed portion of the Railroad will be given to Laborers and all Settling on the Lands of the Company.

At Duluth *Emigrants* and their families will find *free* quarters in a new and commodious *Emigrant House,* until they locate themselves, by applying at Duluth to LUKE MARVIN, Agent. *Laborers* will report to WM. BRANCH, Contractor of the Road. For information as to Steamers to Duluth, inquire at Transportation Office in any of the Lake Cities.

DULUTH, MINN., JUNE 14, 1869.   "DULUTH MINNESOTIAN" PRINT.

Settlers were attracted to Minnesota by newspaper advertisements offering jobs and land.

The Kensington Runestone

In the late 1800s, a Swedish immigrant farmer named Olaf Ohman and his son found a huge stone buried on their farm in central Minnesota. A message was carved on the stone in mysterious markings, called runes.

Language experts came to Minnesota to study the stone. Some of the experts said that the message told of Vikings who came from Sweden and Norway to explore the area in 1362.

Many scholars think the rock is a fake because the wording is not typical of the language in the 1300s. But if the story is true, the stone would prove that Vikings explored Minnesota 130 years before Columbus came to America.

Located near the site where the stone was found, the city of Alexandria, Minnesota, displays the Kensington Runestone in a museum. Alexandria claims to be the Birthplace of America.

Pioneer women in Minnesota did many household jobs, including churning butter *(below)*. In the late 1800s, swarms of grasshoppers invaded Minnesota *(right)*. Some farmers used nets to trap the insects.

Farming was hard work. Families plowed the land, then planted and harvested crops. They repaired tools and buildings and tended the animals. The women usually sewed and mended clothes, canned and cooked food, looked after the children, and made candles and soap.

Sometimes unexpected hardships burdened families. Between 1873 and 1877, billions of grasshoppers ate up most of the crops in southwestern Minnesota. Many farmers gave up and left their farms. Others sent family members to work in logging camps or on farms untouched by the insects.

Even after the grasshoppers left, the high cost of shipping crops by railroad kept farm profits low. Farmers banded together to learn better ways to raise crops and animals. They also worked to get laws passed that could help farmers in need.

By the 1880s, Saint Paul had become a major railroad hub for the Upper Midwest. Trains from as far away as the Pacific Coast made stops at the Saint Paul depot. From southern and western Minnesota and from North and South Dakota, trains brought wheat to Minneapolis to be ground into flour at the city's flour mills.

Logs were carried from lumber camps to sawmills on trains.

An iron mine near Hibbing, in northeastern Minnesota

Iron ore was first mined in northeastern Minnesota in 1884. The ore was shipped by rail to Duluth. There, it was loaded onto ships to cross the Great Lakes to the steel mills in Pennsylvania.

The outbreak of World War I in 1914 brought a demand for Minnesota's products. Wheat was sent overseas to feed soldiers, and iron ore was needed to make guns. During and after the war, the state prospered. But in the 1930s, during the Great Depression, farm prices fell and factory work slowed. Nearly 70 percent of the state's miners lost their jobs.

Tall Tales

One of the best-known heroes of American folklore is the towering lumberjack known as Paul Bunyan. Many stories about Paul Bunyan and his giant blue ox, Babe, take place in Minnesota.

Babe was a big help around Minnesota's logging camps. He could haul a whole forest of logs in one load and break up logjams on rivers with a swish of his tail. Legends say that Paul Bunyan scooped out the Great Lakes to provide drinking water for Babe. And when the ox needed new shoes, the blacksmith needed so much iron that a new mine had to be opened in northern Minnesota.

The legend continues in Minnesota for people who visit the Paul Bunyan Center in Brainerd and the huge statues of Paul Bunyan and Babe in Bemidji.

Giant statues of Paul Bunyan and Babe the Blue Ox stand watch in Bemidji, Minnesota.

These students at a Minneapolis elementary school in the 1940s probably only learned about a few aspects of Indian life. Since that time, Minnesotan schools have been trying to teach more about the rich culture of the American Indian peoples.

World War II (1939–1945) again brought a demand for Minnesota's wheat and iron ore. In the 1950s, however, Minnesota's iron ore began to run out. During the next 30 years, mining jobs in the state dropped to very few.

Gradually, new industries such as trucking, chemicals, electronics, computers, and health care sprang up. More and more farmers began using tractors, which could replace several farmhands. Many of these workers moved to Minnesota's cities.

In the 1970s and 1980s, Minnesotans began to look at their past and at their environment. Many old buildings were restored, and social programs were created to aid Native Americans. People began working to clean up rivers and recycle waste. The 1990s brought more partnerships between business and government, as industries worked to control pollution.

In 1998, Minnesotans elected former professional wrestler Jesse Ventura to be their governor. Ventura was the first member of the Reform Party to be elected to a state office.

The 1990s also brought economic prosperity to Minnesota. Workers flocked to the state, especially its cities, to work at high-tech and other jobs. Immigrants from Asia, Africa, and Latin America have begun to make up a larger part of the state's workforce. As Minnesotans moved into the next millennium, they continued their tradition of hard work.

PEOPLE & ECONOMY

Stars of the North

The Dakota Indians called their land *minne sota*, which means "land of sky-tinted waters." Minnesota is known for its many glistening lakes, its cold winters, and its hardy residents.

Most Minnesotans have ancestors from northern Europe. Members of several other ethnic groups live in the state. Latinos make up about 3 percent of Minnesota's population. About 3.4 percent of Minnesotans are African American, and about 3 percent are Asian American.

Native Americans, though few in number, are found mainly in Minnesota's cities or on the state's 11 reservations. The city of Minneapolis has one of the largest Indian populations of any city in the United States.

Minnesotans brave the cold to enjoy the outdoors in winter. A family plays a game of hockey on a lake in Minneapolis *(opposite page),* and a cross-country skier competes in a race near Biwabik *(above).*

Most of the state's 4.9 million people live in cities and towns, many of which are next to water. Minneapolis and Saint Paul, also called the Twin Cities, straddle the Mississippi River. Minneapolis is the state's largest city, followed by Saint Paul, the state capital. Rochester, Saint Cloud, and Duluth are smaller cities. The busiest port on the Great Lakes, Duluth hugs the southwestern tip of Lake Superior.

About half of all Minnesotans live in the Twin Cities and surrounding communities. The state capitol building *(left)* is in Saint Paul. The skyline of Minneapolis continues to change as the city grows *(opposite page)*.

41

An ice sculptor created this ornate carriage for the Saint Paul Winter Carnival, the largest winter celebration in the nation.

The Twin Cities boast many cultural attractions. The Minneapolis Institute of Arts is Minnesota's largest art museum. The Walker Art Center, a museum of modern art, has an outdoor sculpture garden.

More than 100 theater companies perform in the Twin Cities. The Guthrie Theater in Minneapolis has gained a national reputation for its fine plays.

The Children's Theatre Company, also in Minneapolis, gives some of the state's youngest talent a chance to act on a professional stage.

The Ordway Center for the Performing Arts in Saint Paul was designed to meet the needs of a wide range of performing artists. The Saint Paul Chamber Orchestra, the Minnesota Opera, the Minnesota Orchestra, and many other groups appear at the Ordway.

Another Saint Paul attraction is the Science Museum of Minnesota, where exhibits explain the wonders of science and technology. In Duluth, the Canal Park Marine Museum explores the history of commercial fishing in northern Minnesota. The Lake Superior Railroad Museum features old railroad equipment.

Actors from the Children's Theatre Company perform *Cinderella*.

Spectator sports are popular in Minnesota. The Minnesota Twins baseball team and the Minnesota Vikings football team play in the Hubert H. Humphrey Metrodome in Minneapolis. The Minnesota Timberwolves and the Minnesota Lynx shoot baskets at Minneapolis's Target Center. The Minnesota Wild, a professional hockey team, began playing in Saint Paul's Xcel Energy Center in 2000. A popular minor-league baseball team, the Saint Paul Saints, plays at Midway Stadium in Saint Paul.

Sports fans cheer for the Minnesota Vikings *(above)* and the Minnesota Wild *(right)*.

Split Rock Lighthouse *(left)* guided ships along Lake Superior's rocky shores for over 60 years. The lighthouse later became part of a state park. It features exhibits about Lake Superior's history. Two young fishers show off their catch *(below)*.

The University of Minnesota's teams, all called Golden Gophers, add to the state's sports action. The University of Minnesota-Twin Cities, with about 45,000 students, is one of the largest universities in the nation.

For many Minnesotans, summer means going to the lake. Minnesota's lakes and rivers lure people to the water to swim, canoe, sail, and water-ski. Long winters encourage skiing, ice-skating, sledding, and ice fishing. Minnesota has 70 state parks and 58 state forests for outdoor recreation.

Though no longer Minnesota's main industries, farming and mining are still important to the state. But both industries have changed greatly. Farmers and miners use computers and other modern equipment such as trucks, tractors, conveyor belts, and bulldozers to do the work with fewer people.

Only about 4 percent of Minnesota's population works in the agriculture industry. Still, the state's

farms produce much of the milk, butter, eggs, turkeys, grains, and some of the vegetables that Americans buy. Major crops include soybeans, corn, hay, potatoes, wheat, and peas. Minnesota's livestock supply dairy products, eggs, and meat. Apples grow well in southern Minnesota.

Mining continues in Minnesota but with fewer jobs than it had during the 1940s. Minnesota supplies more iron ore than any other state. Manufacturing employs nearly 14 percent of Minnesota's workers. Computers, medical products, Scotch tape, and flour are a few of the many products made in the state.

Wheat *(opposite page)* and apples *(top)* are harvested from Minnesota farms. Lumber for buildings and furniture comes from forests in northern Minnesota *(right)*.

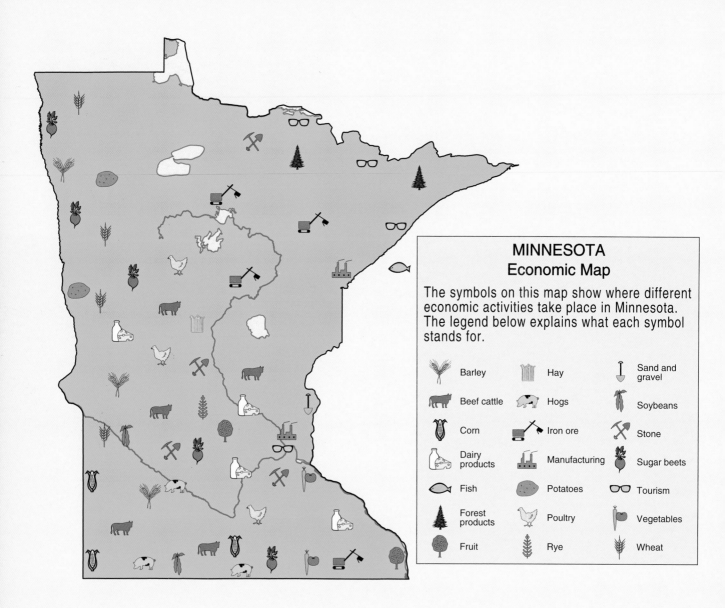

MINNESOTA
Economic Map

The symbols on this map show where different economic activities take place in Minnesota. The legend below explains what each symbol stands for.

Barley		Hay		Sand and gravel	
Beef cattle		Hogs		Soybeans	
Corn		Iron ore		Stone	
Dairy products		Manufacturing		Sugar beets	
Fish		Potatoes		Tourism	
Forest products		Poultry		Vegetables	
Fruit		Rye		Wheat	

A street vendor sells flowers in downtown Minneapolis. Many service workers in Minnesota have jobs in the state's large cities.

Service jobs, most of which have developed since World War II, create about 61 percent of Minnesota's income and employ most of the state's workers. People in service jobs help other people or businesses. Lawyers, store clerks, and bankers are just some of the people who hold service jobs.

Another service industry is medicine. Each year, the Mayo Clinic in Rochester treats thousands of patients. The world-famous clinic has more than 1,200 doctors.

Minnesota earned one of its first nicknames, the Bread and Butter State, back in the 1800s when grains, flour milling, and dairy products helped the state grow. Minnesota is still growing, and its strength in modern businesses such as computers and health care promises a bright future for the state.

THE ENVIRONMENT

Battle over the Boundary Waters

Minnesota is known as the Land of 10,000 Lakes. At least 1,000 of its lakes are found in a northeastern region known as the Boundary Waters Canoe Area Wilderness (BWCAW). The BWCAW is situated along the border between Minnesota and Canada. It lies within the Superior National Forest and covers more than 1 million acres of lakes, rivers, and forests. Many of the lakes are connected, making the region ideal for water recreation. Over 200,000 visitors come to the BWCAW to camp, hike, boat, and canoe every year.

As its name says, the BWCAW is a wilderness. The federal government defines **wilderness area** as a designated natural place where people cannot

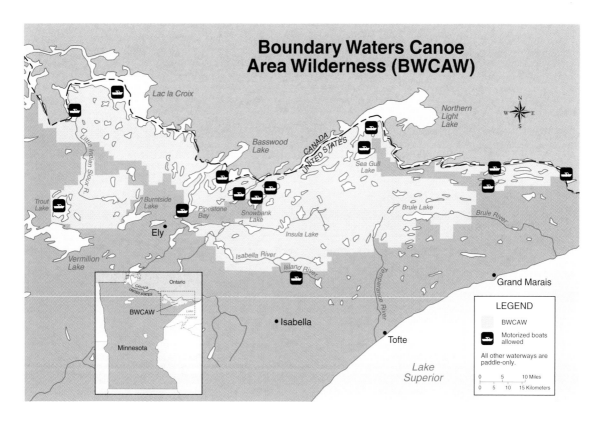

Boundary Waters Canoe Area Wilderness (BWCAW)

Lac la Croix

Northern Light Lake

Basswood Lake

CANADA / UNITED STATES

Sea Gull Lake

Little Indian Sioux R.

Trout Lake

Burntside Lake

Pipestone Bay

Snowbank Lake

Brule Lake

Brule River

Ely

Insula Lake

Vermilion Lake

Isabella River

Island River

Temperance River

Grand Marais

Ontario

CANADA / UNITED STATES

BWCAW

Lake Superior

Minnesota

Isabella

Tofte

Lake Superior

LEGEND

BWCAW

Motorized boats allowed

All other waterways are paddle-only.

0   5   10 Miles
0   5   10   15 Kilometers

disturb the environment. The federal government protects the BWCAW and other wilderness areas and makes sure that people do not alter them. In the BWCAW, there are no roads or power lines and few signs of modern technology. Motorboats, snowmobiles, cars, and trucks are not allowed in most parts of the wilderness area.

The Boundary Waters Canoe Area Wilderness is in northeastern Minnesota along the Canadian border *(above)*. It is a favorite destination for canoeists *(opposite page)*.

But the BWCAW is not always a quiet place. The area has often been disturbed by disagreements about the way the land and water should be used by people and industries. Since the 1920s, Minnesotans and visitors have argued over whether the area should be developed or remain wild.

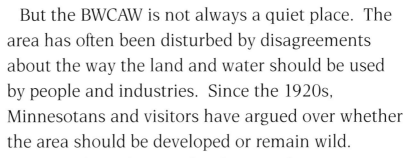

Fur trappers were among the early white settlers in northern Minnesota.

The Dakota and Ojibway Indians were some of the earliest residents of what later became the BWCAW. During the 1600s and 1700s, fur traders and explorers lived and worked in the region. In the late 1800s and early 1900s, the land was used for mining and logging.

In 1909 President Theodore Roosevelt approved the creation of the Superior National Forest. After World War I, many nature lovers began vacationing there, boating on the lakes near the Canadian border. Resorts opened and roads were built.

Some Minnesotans believed that the increasing numbers of visitors were ruining the area. In 1926 the federal government

decided to create a "roadless area," a part of the Superior National Forest where no roads could be built. The roadless area was enlarged during the 1930s. By 1939 it covered more than 1 million acres.

People kept visiting the roadless area, attracted by its natural beauty. By the 1940s, visitors were flying to the resorts, since they couldn't drive there. The airplanes, which landed on lakes, were very loud. In 1949 airplanes were banned from the roadless area. And in 1958 the roadless area was renamed the Boundary Waters Canoe Area (BWCA).

Campers in the Superior National Forest load up their canoe in 1930. The area has been a popular vacation spot for Minnesotans since the early 1900s.

Congress passed the Wilderness Act, creating the National Wilderness Preservation System, in 1964. This law defined a wilderness area as a place that is not disturbed by people. It also set aside 54 wilderness areas across the country to be part of the National Wilderness Preservation System. The BWCA was one of the official wilderness areas. According to the new law, logging and motor use were restricted in the wilderness areas. Still, in the BWCA, logging continued to be allowed, and people continued to travel in motorboats and snowmobiles.

Environmentalists wanted to make sure the BWCA was not used in ways that violated rules for wilderness areas. In 1978 the U.S. Congress passed the BWCA Wilderness Act, a law saying that the BWCA could not be developed anymore. That made logging and mining illegal in the area. In addition, motorized vehicles were banned from most parts of the park. Most visitors to the BWCA would have to travel by canoe or on foot. Also, the name of the area was changed to the Boundary Waters Canoe Area Wilderness.

Some residents of towns near the BWCAW did not like the new law. They thought that the BWCAW did not fit the definition of a wilderness area because the land had been used and developed by people for many years. They felt that the government had taken away their control of the economy. Loggers and miners lost their jobs. Many northeastern Minnesotans earned a living from the motorboaters and snowmobilers who came to the BWCAW. These people thought everyone should have access to the area—not just canoeists.

Over time, Minnesotans in towns near the BWCAW have learned to profit from visiting canoeists. They have set up outdoor supply stores and other businesses that serve tourists. But some people continue to work for more development of the BWCAW.

Tourists prepare to head into the BWCAW with gear and a guide from Ely, Minnesota.

Visitors to the BWCAW are allowed to use vehicles to haul their boats over some portages. These canoeists are doing the job on foot.

In 1998 a law was passed that allowed cars and trucks to haul boats over certain portages, or land between lakes, in the BWCAW. Many environmentalists opposed the law. They worry that cars and trucks will pollute the air and disturb the area's wildlife and its natural beauty. With cars and trucks in the area, it will not truly be a wilderness. Other people say the law is practical. Cars and trucks are needed to pull canoes from one place to another.

The debate over the use of the Boundary Waters continues. Some people want to ban completely all motorized vehicles to preserve the wilderness. Others want to open it up to more people and development. Minnesotans must decide how they will keep their natural areas clean and meet the needs of the people at the same time.

Minnesotans want vacationers to enjoy the Boundary Waters area without disturbing its natural beauty.

Fun Facts

During winter, the town of International Falls in northern Minnesota often records the coldest daily temperature in the continental United States.

Although Minnesota is sometimes called the Land of 10,000 Lakes, there are actually about 15,291 lakes in the state. Of those lakes, 11,842 are over 10 acres in size. Lakes cover 4,750 square miles of Minnesota, or 5 percent of the state's area.

There are over 500 stores in the Mall of America in Bloomington, Minnesota. If a shopper spent 10 minutes in every store in the mall, he or she would be there for about 84 hours.

Every year, Minnesota anglers catch more than 3.5 million walleyes weighing a total of about 4 million pounds.

In-line skates were developed in Minnesota by Scott Olson, a former hockey player who wanted to be able to practice skating year-round.

Waterskiing was invented on Lake Pepin in southeastern Minnesota in 1922.

During the 1930s, Saint Paul, Minnesota, was a hideout for many gangsters, including John Dillinger and George "Baby Face" Nelson.

The northernmost point in the United States (outside of Alaska) is located in Minnesota.

In-line skating is popular not only in Minnesota, where in-line skates were invented, but also throughout the United States.

STATE SONG

"Hail! Minnesota" was written by two students at the University of Minnesota in 1904 and 1905. It was adopted as the official state song of Minnesota in 1945.

HAIL! MINNESOTA

Music by Truman E. Rickard; lyrics by Truman E. Rickard and Arthur E. Upson

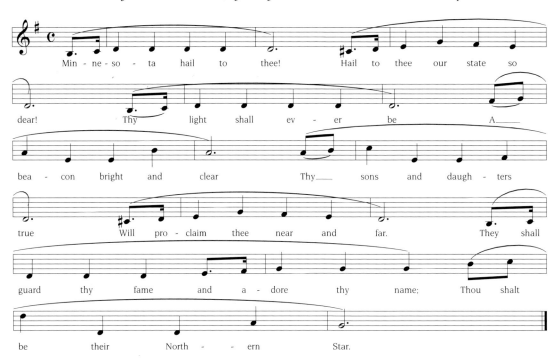

You can hear "Hail! Minnesota" by visiting this website:
<http://www.state.mn.us/aam/aamp5-6.html#song>

A MINNESOTA RECIPE

Wild rice grows in water, so it thrives in the Land of 10,000 Lakes, where 1 million pounds are harvested each year. Minnesota is one of two states to grow wild rice commercially. Use vegetable broth and leave out the chicken in this recipe for a vegetarian delight.

WILD RICE CHICKEN SOUP

½ cup butter
1 finely chopped onion
½ cup chopped celery
½ cup sliced carrots
½ pound sliced mushrooms
¾ cup all-purpose flour
6 cups chicken broth
2 cups cooked wild rice

1 pound cubed, cooked chicken
½ teaspoon salt
½ teaspoon curry powder
½ teaspoon mustard powder
½ teaspoon dried parsley
½ teaspoon ground black pepper
1 cup slivered almonds
2 cups half-and-half

1. Over medium heat, melt butter in large saucepan. Ask an adult for help.
2. Add onion, carrots, and celery. Stir, and sauté for 5 minutes.
3. Add mushrooms and sauté for 2 additional minutes.
4. Add flour and stir vigorously.
5. Stirring constantly, pour in chicken broth.
6. Bring mixture to boil, then reduce heat to low and allow to simmer.
7. Add rice, salt, curry powder, chicken, parsley, mustard powder, almonds, and ground black pepper. Allow to heat thoroughly, then add half-and-half.
8. Let entire mixture simmer for 1 to 2 hours. Serve hot. Makes 8 to 10 servings.

HISTORICAL TIMELINE

8000 B.C. Indians begin moving into Minnesota.

A.D. 1500 Dakota Indians construct homes and begin to hunt.

1650s French explorers visit Lake Superior.

1680 Louis Hennepin names the Falls of Saint Anthony.

1736 Ojibway and Dakota Indians begin fighting over land in northern Minnesota.

1803 The Louisiana Purchase, which includes most of Minnesota, doubles the size of the United States.

1805 Zebulon Pike trades with Dakota Indians for land.

1820 Construction of Fort Snelling begins.

1837 Dakota and Ojibway Indians sell land east of the Mississippi River to the U.S. government.

1849 Saint Paul becomes the capital of the Minnesota Territory.

1851 The Dakota sell most of southern Minnesota to the U.S. government.

1854–55 The Ojibway sign over most of northern Minnesota to the U.S. government.

1858 Minnesota becomes the 32nd state.

1862 Little Crow leads the Dakota in an uprising against Minnesota settlers.

1873–77 Grasshoppers destroy crops in southwestern Minnesota.

1884 The mining of iron ore begins in northeastern Minnesota.

1929 The Great Depression begins. Farm prices fall, and Minnesota's mining industry slows.

1987 The State of Minnesota and the Dakota Indians declare a Year of Reconciliation.

1998 Minnesotans elect Jesse Ventura, the first Reform Party governor in the United States.

2001 Spring floods cause damage estimated at $10 million.

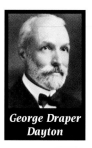

George Draper Dayton

OUTSTANDING MINNESOTANS

Elmer L. Andersen (born 1909) was elected governor of Minnesota in 1960. In 1941 he began running the adhesives company H. B. Fuller. Andersen has made countless charitable donations and is one of the most important collectors of rare books in the United States.

Ann Bancroft (born 1955) is a pioneering polar explorer. In 1986, she became the first woman to reach the North Pole by traveling across the ice. In 2001 she and Liv Arneson became the first women to cross the entire continent of Antarctica. Bancroft lives in Scandia.

Bob Dylan

George Draper Dayton (1857–1938) moved to Minnesota from New York in 1883. In 1902 he opened a department store in Minneapolis. By 2000 the Minneapolis-based Target Corporation was one of the largest retailers in the United States.

Bob Dylan (born 1941) grew up in Hibbing, Minnesota. Dylan, a songwriter and singer known especially for his protest lyrics, influenced folk and rock music during the 1960s and 1970s.

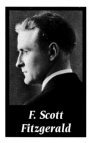

F. Scott Fitzgerald

F. Scott Fitzgerald (1896–1940), born in Saint Paul, is famous for his novels that are set in the 1920s. His books include *This Side of Paradise* and *The Great Gatsby.*

Wanda Gág (1893–1946), from New Ulm, was a writer and illustrator of award-winning children's books. She is best remembered for the classic *Millions of Cats.*

Judy Garland (1922–1969), a singer and actress, is best remembered as Dorothy in *The Wizard of Oz.* She also starred in *Meet Me in St. Louis* and *Easter Parade.* She was born in Grand Rapids, Minnesota.

Judy Garland

Hubert H. Humphrey (1911–1978) served as a U.S. senator from Minnesota for 23 years. While in the Senate, he introduced a bill to establish the Peace Corps, and he fought for passage of the 1964 Civil Rights Act. Humphrey was vice president of the United States from 1965 to 1969 and ran unsuccessfully for president in 1968.

Hubert H. Humphrey

Garrison Keillor (born 1942) became widely known for his stories about Lake Wobegon on the radio program *A Prairie Home Companion.* A native of Anoka, Minnesota, Keillor also writes humorous books and magazine articles.

Garrison Keillor

Elizabeth Kenny (1880–1952) was a nurse who moved from Australia to Minnesota in 1940. Kenny developed a method to treat victims of poliomyelitis, a virus that weakens muscles and sometimes causes them to stop working. Kenny's work pioneered the field of physical therapy.

Jessica Lange (born 1949) is an actress from Cloquet, Minnesota. She has won Academy Awards for her roles in *Tootsie* and *Blue Sky.* She spends part of her time at her home in Stillwater, Minnesota.

Sinclair Lewis

Sinclair Lewis (1885–1951) was a writer and the first American to be awarded the Nobel Prize for literature. His hometown, Sauk Centre, Minnesota, was the model for his most famous book, *Main Street.*

Charles Lindbergh (1902–1974) was an aviator who grew up in Little Falls, Minnesota. In 1927 he became the first person to fly solo across the Atlantic Ocean. His book about the flight, titled *The Spirit of St. Louis,* won a Pulitzer Prize in 1954.

Charles Lindbergh

Charles Mayo

William Mayo

Walter Mondale

Jeanette Piccard

Charles Horace Mayo (1865–1939) and **William James Mayo** (1861–1939) helped establish a medical center that grew to be the widely famed Mayo Clinic in Rochester, Minnesota. The brothers also founded the Mayo Foundation for Medical Education and Research.

Eugene McCarthy (born 1916) was a politician. Born in Watkins, he worked as a teacher before serving Minnesota in the U.S. House of Representatives and the U.S. Senate. He was a strong critic of United States involvement in the Vietnam War. In 1968 he ran unsuccessfully for president.

William McKnight (1887–1978) took a job in 1907 with 3M's sandpaper factory in Duluth, Minnesota. Just nine years later, he became president of 3M, and for the next 50 years he led the company to become an international giant.

Kevin McHale (born 1957) was a basketball player who grew up in Hibbing and played for the University of Minnesota Golden Gophers. He was a forward for the Boston Celtics from 1980 until 1993, and he helped them win three NBA championships. In 1995 he returned to his home state to work as an executive for the Minnesota Timberwolves.

Walter Mondale (born 1928), a native of Elmore, Minnesota, served as a U.S. senator for 12 years. He was vice president of the United States from 1977 to 1981. In 1984 Mondale ran for president but did not win the election.

Jeanette Piccard (1895–1981) was born in Chicago but lived in Minneapolis much of her life. In 1934 she became the first woman to pilot a hot-air balloon to the stratosphere, an upper layer of the earth's atmosphere.

Prince (born 1958), whose original name is Prince Rogers Nelson, grew up in Minneapolis. A pop singer, songwriter, and musician, he has made many albums and several films, including *Purple Rain*. He has his own studio, Paisley Park, in Chanhassen, Minnesota, and his own record label.

Prince

Winona Ryder (born 1971) was named after the Minnesota town where she was born, Winona. The actress has starred in movies including *Beetlejuice*, *Heathers*, and *Girl, Interrupted*. She was nominated for Academy Awards for her roles in *Little Women* and *The Age of Innocence.*

Charles Schulz (1922–2000) created the "Peanuts" comic strip and drew it for fifty years. "Peanuts" is found in more than 6,000 newspapers around the world. Schulz was born in Minneapolis and grew up in Saint Paul.

Charles Schulz

Will Steger (born 1945) became famous in 1986 when he made a trek by dog sled to the North Pole. In 1990 he participated in the first trip across Antarctica's greatest width—3,741 miles. He also crossed the Arctic Ocean from Russia to Canada in 1995.

Will Steger

Harold Stassen (1907–2001) became governor of Minnesota in 1938 at age 31, making him the youngest governor ever in the United States. In 1945 Stassen helped found the United Nations. He was a frequent but unsuccessful candidate for national political office.

Jesse Ventura (born 1951) made political history in 1998 as the nation's first Reform Party candidate to be elected governor. Before his election to Minnesota's highest office, Ventura was a Navy SEAL, a professional wrestler, radio host, and a suburban mayor. He was born and grew up in Minneapolis.

Jesse Ventura

FACTS-AT-A-GLANCE

Nickname: The North Star State; Land of 10,000 Lakes

Song: "Hail! Minnesota"

Motto: *L'Etoile du Nord* (The Star of the North)

Flower: pink and white lady's slipper

Tree: Norway pine

Bird: common loon

Fish: walleye

Grain: wild rice

Gemstone: Lake Superior agate

Drink: milk

Date and ranking of statehood: May 11, 1858, the 32nd state

Capital: Saint Paul

Area: 79,617 square miles

Rank in area, nationwide: 14th

Average January temperature: 8° F

Average July temperature: 70° F

The Minnesota state flag shows the state flower, the lady's slipper, a farmer plowing a field, and a Native American riding a horse toward the setting sun.

POPULATION GROWTH

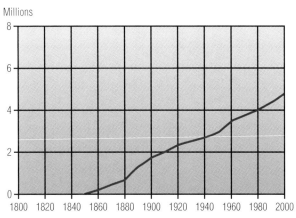

Millions

This chart shows how Minnesota's population has grown from 1850 to 2000.

Minnesota's state seal shows a farmer plowing a field, a stump to represent the lumber industry, and an Indian riding by on a horse to represent the state's heritage. The scene is set near the Falls of Saint Anthony on the Mississippi River.

Population: 4,919,479 (2000 census)

Rank in population, nationwide: 21st

Major cities and populations: (2000 census) Minneapolis (382,618), Saint Paul (287,151), Duluth (86,918), Rochester (85,806), Bloomington (85,172)

U.S. senators: 2

U.S. representatives: 8

Electoral votes: 10

Natural resources: fertile soil, forests, granite, iron ore, lakes and rivers, limestone, manganese, peat, sand and gravel, sandstone, taconite

Agricultural products: apples, barley, beef cattle, carrots, corn, eggs, green peas, hay, hogs, milk, onions, potatoes, rye, soybeans, sugar beets, turkeys, wheat

Fishing industry: buffalo fish, carp, catfish, lake herring, smelt, walleye, whitefish, yellow perch, yellow pike

Manufactured goods: computers and computer equipment, flour, machinery, medical products, metal products, paper products, printed materials, scientific instruments

WHERE MINNESOTANS WORK

Services—65 percent (services includes jobs in trade; community, social, and personal services; finance, insurance, and real estate; transportation, communication, and utilities)

Manufacturing—14 percent

Government—12 percent

Construction—5 percent

Agriculture—4 percent

Mining—less than 1 percent

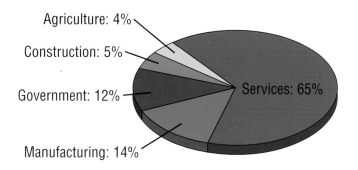

GROSS STATE PRODUCT

Services—61 percent

Manufacturing—19 percent

Government—11 percent

Agriculture—4 percent

Construction—4 percent

Mining—1 percent

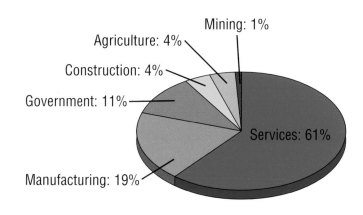

MINNESOTA WILDLIFE

Mammals: bat, beaver, black bear, bobcat, fox, gopher, mink, moose, muskrat, otter, rabbit, raccoon, skunk, squirrel, weasel, white-tailed deer, wolf

Birds: blue jay, cardinal, crow, duck, loon, quail, ring-necked pheasant, robin, sparrow, woodpecker

Reptiles and amphibians: frogs, newt, northern prairie skink, salamander, snakes, six-lined racerunner, toads, turtles

Fish: bass, muskellunge, northern pike, sunfish, trout, walleye

Trees: ash, aspen, balsam fir, black walnut, elm, maple, oak, pine, spruce, white birch

Wild plants: aster, bird's foot violet, blazing star, blueberry, goldenrod, honeysuckle, prairie phlox, wild geranium, wild rose

The gopher is the mascot of the University of Minnesota.

PLACES TO VISIT

Boundary Waters Canoe Area Wilderness, northeastern Minnesota

Part of the Superior National Forest, the BWCAW is a large network of lakes and streams located along the border between Minnesota and Canada. Canoeists from near and far flock to the BWCAW for its peace and natural beauty.

Canal Park, Duluth

This park sits next to the canal that leads to Duluth's busy harbor on Lake Superior. Visitors can watch ships on the lake or stop by the Lake Superior Maritime Visitor Center to learn about ships, sailors, and life on the largest Great Lake.

Gooseberry Falls State Park, near Two Harbors

This popular state park is located next to Lake Superior and the Gooseberry River. Visiting waterfalls on the river, hiking, camping, and swimming are some of the activities available.

Great Lakes Aquarium, Duluth

Open since 2000, this is the first all-freshwater aquarium in the United States. The aquarium, located next to Lake Superior, displays Great Lakes wildlife in natural habitat exhibits.

Historic Fort Snelling, Saint Paul

Built in the 1820s where the Mississippi and Minnesota Rivers meet, Fort Snelling has been restored to its appearance in 1827. Visitors to the living museum interact with soldiers, fur traders, craftspeople, and other workers in their historic surroundings.

Ironworld Discovery Center, near Chisholm
The center celebrates the history of miners in the region of Minnesota called the Iron Range. Explore an open pit mine, tour a restored miner's home, or study mining exhibits.

Itasca State Park
The mighty Mississippi River flows out of Lake Itasca. Visitors can walk across the Mississippi on stepping stones at its source. Minnesota's oldest state park is also home to other lakes, forests, and hiking trails.

Mall of America, Bloomington
The largest mall in the United States attracts millions of visitors from all over the world each year. It features over 500 stores, restaurants and bars, movie theaters, an indoor amusement park, an aquarium, a wedding chapel, a Lego play area, and more.

Science Museum of Minnesota, Saint Paul
Budding scientists and grown-ups alike can conduct hands-on experiments, see a 3D laser show, or navigate a virtual towboat on the Mississippi River. The museum features activities and exhibits about human biology, natural history, technology, and other areas of science.

Walker Art Center, Minneapolis
This museum focuses on modern art in its many forms. The Minneapolis Sculpture Garden is located next to the art center and is home to the Spoonbridge and Cherry sculpture, a popular Minneapolis symbol.

A girl climbs over rocks at the origin of the Mississippi River in Itasca State Park.

ANNUAL EVENTS

Saint Paul Winter Carnival—*January*

John Beargrease Sled Dog Race, near Duluth—*January*

Ice Box Days, International Falls—*January*

International Eelpout Festival, Walker—*February*

Heart of the Beast May Day Parade, Minneapolis—*May*

Cinco de Mayo, Saint Paul—*May*

Scottish Country Fair, Saint Paul—*May*

Grand Old Day, Saint Paul—*June*

Grandma's Marathon, Duluth—*June*

Aquatennial Festival, Minneapolis—*July*

Fisherman's Picnic, Grand Marais—*July*

Defeat of Jesse James Days, Northfield—*September*

Oktoberfest, New Ulm—*October*

Holidazzle Parades, Minneapolis—*November–December*

LEARN MORE ABOUT MINNESOTA

BOOKS

General

Carlson, Jeffrey D. *A Historical Album of Minnesota.* Brookfield, CT: The Millbrook Press, 1993.

Fradin, Dennis Brindell and Judith Bloom Fradin. *Minnesota.* Chicago: Children's Press, 1996.

Hintz, Martin. *Minnesota.* Danbury, CT: Children's Press, 2000. For older readers.

Thompson, Kathleen. *Minnesota.* Austin, TX: Raintree/Steck Vaughn, 1996.

Special Interest

Crofford, Emily. *Frontier Surgeons: A Story about the Mayo Brothers.* Minneapolis, MN: Carolrhoda Books, Inc., 1989. A biography of William and Charles Mayo, the brothers who pioneered new techniques in surgery and founded the world-famous Mayo Clinic in Rochester.

Crofford, Emily. *Healing Warrior: A Story about Sister Elizabeth Kenny.* Minneapolis, MN: Carolrhoda Books, Inc., 1989. Crofford tells the surprising story of the self-taught nurse whose new treatment helped thousands overcome polio.

Paulsen, Gary. *Woodsong.* Reprint edition. New York: Puffin, 1991. An award-winning Minnesota author describes his relationship with the state's north woods, where he trained a dog-sled team for a race in Alaska.

Regguinti, Gordon. *The Sacred Harvest: Ojibway Wild Rice Gathering.* Minneapolis, MN: Lerner Publications Company, 1992. This photoessay follows an 11-year-old Ojibway boy in northern Minnesota, as he goes with his father to harvest wild rice for the first time.

Fiction

Marvin, Isabel R. *A Bride for Anna's Papa.* Minneapolis, MN: Milkweed Editions, 1994. After Anna's mother dies, she and her brother hope to find a new wife for their father in this novel set in a small Minnesota town in the early 1900s.

Paulsen, Gary. *The Winter Room.* Reprint edition. New York: Bantam Books, 1998. In this Newbery Honor-winning novel, Paulsen tells the story of Eldon and Wayne, who discover an important truth about their uncle on a Minnesota farm in the 1930s.

Schultz, Jan Neubert. *Horse Sense: The Story of Will Sasse, His Horse Star, and the Outlaw Jesse James.* Minneapolis, MN: Carolrhoda Books, Inc., 2001. Schultz tells the story of the James gang's raid and bank heist in Northfield, Minnesota, in 1876.

Wilder, Laura Ingalls. *On the Banks of Plum Creek.* New York: HarperCollins, 1953. The beloved children's author tells the story of the Ingalls' battle with a blizzard and a plague of grasshoppers in Minnesota in the 1870s.

WEBSITES

North Star—Minnesota State Government Online
<http://www.state.mn.us/>
Minnesota's official website features information for tourists,
government news, and a directory of state offices.

Explore Minnesota
<http://www.exploreminnesota.com>
Visit this detailed site for up-to-date information on outdoor fun,
tourist attractions, and festivals.

Native Peoples of Minnesota
<http://emuseum.mnsu.edu/history/mncultures/index.shtml>
Learn about the history and culture of Minnesota's first
inhabitants.

Science Museum of Minnesota
<http://www.smm.org>
Take a virtual tour of the state's largest science museum and
try out interactive games and experiments that relate to the
museum's exhibits.

Startribune.com
<http://www.startribune.com>
Read about current events in the online version of the *Star Tribune*,
a popular Minnesota newspaper.

PRONUNCIATION GUIDE

Chouart des Groseilliers, Médard
(shwar day groh-zeh-YAY, MAY-dahr)

Duluth (duh-LOOTH)

Hennepin, Louis (HEHN-uh-pihn,
LOO-ee)

Iroquois (IHR-uh-kwoy)

Itasca (eye-TAS-kuh)

Minneapolis (mihn-ee-AP-uh-luhs)

Ojibway (oh-JIHB-way)

Radisson, Pierre Esprit (RA-dih-suhn,
pee-AYR ehs-PREE)

Saint Croix (saynt KROY)

Sioux (SOO)

GLOSSARY

bluff: a steep, high bank, found especially along a river; a cliff

drift: a mixture of clay, sand, gravel, and boulders deposited by a glacier, plus any materials added to this mixture by the running water of a melting glacier

glacier: a large body of ice and snow that moves slowly over land

Great Lakes: a chain of five lakes in Canada and the northern United States. They are Lakes Superior, Michigan, Huron, Erie, and Ontario.

ice age: a period when ice sheets cover large regions of the earth. The term *Ice Age* usually refers to the most recent one, called the Pleistocene, which began almost 2 million years ago.

immigrant: a person who moves to a foreign country and settles there

missionary: a person sent out by a religious group to spread its beliefs to other people

reservation: public land set aside by the government to be used by Native Americans

treaty: an agreement between two or more groups, usually having to do with peace or trade

wetland: a swamp, marsh, or other low, wet area that often borders a river, lake, or ocean

wilderness area: land protected by the U.S. government where people do not live or work. These areas are not allowed to be developed by people so that they stay as natural as possible. There are 644 wilderness areas in the United States.

INDEX

PHOTO ACKNOWLEDGMENTS

Cover photographs by © Bill Ross/CORBIS (right) and © Richard Hamilton Smith/CORBIS (left); Digital Cartographics, pp. 1, 8, 9, 48, 51; Richard Hamilton Smith/CORBIS, pp. 2–3; Layne Kennedy/CORBIS, pp. 3, 6, 56; Louise K. Broman/Root Resources, pp. 4, 7 (detail), 17 (detail), 38 (detail), 50 (detail); Lynn M. Stone, pp. 7, 15, 16; Kay Shaw, pp. 10, 11, 25, 42, 69 (second from bottom), 80; Jim Simondet/IPS, pp. 12, 45 (bottom); Richard Thom/Visuals Unlimited, p. 13; Lucille Sukalo, pp. 14 (both), 47 (both); Emily Slowinski, p. 17; John Polis, p. 18; National Archives of Canada, Ottawa, p. 19 (C-114467 – detail); Minnesota Historical Society, pp. 20, 21, 26, 27, 29, 30, 32 (top), 33, 53; Len Rue, Jr./Visuals Unlimited, p. 22; Northwest Magazine, p. 23; Library of Congress, p. 24; National Anthropological Archives, Smithsonian Institution, p. 28; Viking Research, Bill Holman, Alexandria, Minnesota, p. 31; Minneapolis Public Library and Information Center, pp. 32 (bottom), 34; © Phil Schermeister/CORBIS, pp. 35, 75; Independent Picture Service, pp. 36, 68 (second from bottom); Todd Strand/IPS, p. 38; © Richard Hamilton Smith/CORBIS, pp. 39, 61; Karen Sirvaitis, pp. 40, 49; © Joseph Sohm, ChromoSohm, Inc./CORBIS, p. 41; Greater Minneapolis Convention & Visitors Association, p. 43; © AFP/CORBIS, p. 44 (left); Elsa Hasch/Allsport, p. 44 (right); James Blank/Root Resources, p. 45 (top); Harvest States Cooperatives, St. Paul, Minnesota, p. 46; © Michael S. Yamashita/CORBIS, p. 50; Denver Public Library, Western History Department, p. 52; © Ed Wargin/CORBIS, p. 54; © Bob Krist/CORBIS, pp. 57, 58–59; Jack Lindstrom, p. 60; Tim Seeley, pp. 63, 71, 72; Dayton Hudson Corporation, p. 66 (top); John Rott, News-Tribune & Herald, Duluth, Minnesota, p. 66 (second from top); Charles Scribner's Sons, p. 66 (second from bottom); Hollywood Book & Poster Co., p. 66 (bottom), 69 (top); Marty Nordstrom, Minnesota Historical Society, p. 67 (top); Will Crockett, Minnesota Public Radio, p. 67 (second from top); Sinclair Lewis Foundation, Inc., p. 67 (second from bottom); Courtesy of ASME via National Air and Space Museum, Smithsonian Institution (SI neg. #86-13507), p. 67 (bottom); Mayo Foundation Historical Collection, p. 68 (top, second from top); Dearborn Historical Museum, p. 68 (bottom); Roddy McDowall, p. 69 (second from top); State of Minnesota, Office of the Governor-Elect, p. 69 (bottom); Jean Matheny, p. 70; © Gunter Marx Photography/CORBIS, p. 73.